YOU ARE A LION

30 Days to Unlocking Your Inner Roar

By Raimele Reese

COPYRIGHT 2021 ICHAMPION PUBLISHING

ALL RIGHT RESERVED. NO PORTION OF THIS BOOK MAY BE REPRODUCED, SCANNED, STORED IN A RETRIEVAL SYSTEM, TRANSMITTED IN ANY FORM OR BY ANY MEANS- ELECTRONICALLY, MECHANICALLY, PHOTOCOPY, RECORDING OR ANY OTHER- EXCEPT FOR BRIEF QUOTATIONS IN PRINTED REVIEWS, WITHOUT WRITTEN PERMISSION OF THE PUBLISHER. PLEASE DO NOT PARTICIPATE OR ENCOURAGE PIRACY OR COPYRIGHTED MATERIALS IN VIOLATION OF THE AUTHOR'S RIGHTS. PURCHASE ONLY AUTHORIZED EDITIONS.

PUBLISHED BY ICHAMPION PUBLISHING
P.O. BOX 2352 FRISCO, TX 75034
CONTENT EDIT BY NIKIA HAMMONDS-BLAKELY AND ICHAMPION PUBLISHING
LIBRARY OF CONGRESS CATALOGING-IN-PUBLICATION DATA PUBLISHER AND PRINTING BY ICHAMPION PUBLISHING

WRITTEN BY: RAMIELE REESE
COVER DESIGN BY: ICHAMPION PUBLISHING
YOU ARE A LION
ISBN: 978-1-7362684-3-8

CATEGORIES:
SELF-HELP TECHNIQUES
SPIRITUALITY

UNLESS OTHERWISE NOTED, ALL SCRIPTURE QUOTATIONS ARE FROM THE NEW KING JAMES VERSION OF THE
BIBLE. NIV, AMP, MSG ESV VERSIONS ALSO FEATURED. COPYRIGHT 1979, 1980 & 1982 BY THOMAS NELSON, INC., PUBLISHERS.

You Are A Lion

30 Days to Unlocking Your Inner Roar

THIS JOURNAL IS ESPECIALLY FOR:

FROM:

NEW JOURNEY THOUGHTS

Write about what you are expecting to:
See, Feel, Encounter, Change, and more while embarking on this
New 30 Day Journey of "Letting Your Roar Be Heard"

DATE:

Day 1

THE BRIGHT SIDE OF IT...

God Is Still Able
You're Still Here
You Can Make It
You Can Keep Your Hand In His Hand

YOUR THOUGHTS

BACKUP POWER: PSALM 121:1-3 NIV

Scripture: Psalm 121:3

I lift up my eyes to the mountains- where does my help come from? My help comes from the Lord, the Maker of Heaven and Earth. He will not let your foot slip- he who watches over you will not slumber.

What is keeping you from trusting fully?

Day 2

Scripture: Isaiah 40:28-29 NIV

Do you not know? Have you not heard? The Lord is the everlasting God, the Creator of the ends of the earth. He will not grow tired or weary, and his understanding no one can fathom. He gives strength to the weary and increases the power of the weak.

What do you think your superhero powers are?

YOU ARE A SUPERHERO...

*Believe it or not, someone calls you that.
You're stronger than Superman and smarter than Tony Stark.
God has empowered you with greatness, walk in it and watch
God's works come through you!!!*

YOUR THOUGHTS

BACKUP POWER: ISAIAH 40:28-29 NIV

Day 3

Scripture: John 15:12-13 NLT

This is my commandment: Love each other in the same way I have loved you. There is no greater love than to lay down one's life for one's friends.

Describe a time when you felt pure, genuine, love?

YOU ARE BETTER THAN THINGS...

We can buy things all day, which are temporary.
But genuine love is long-lasting,
the same love God has for us.
Things Don't Supercede Genuine Love!!!

YOUR THOUGHTS

BACKUP POWER: JOHN 15: 12-13 NLT

Day 4

DON'T CHANGE THE COURSE...

*From this day forward,
you will not allow others' nonchalant attitude
toward your Dreams, Goals, etc., to make you change your course.
Trust God that if He gave it to you, He will make a way for it!*

YOUR THOUGHTS

BACKUP POWER: JEREMIAH 29:11 NIV

Scripture: Jeremiah 29:11

For I know the plans I have for you, declares the Lord, plans to prosper you and not to harm you, plans to give you hope and a future.

What's next for you?
Map put your next plans and direction.

_____
_____
_____
_____
_____
_____
_____
_____
_____
_____
_____
_____
_____
_____

Day 5

STAY HUMBLE...

Today Make Sure That Your

"Confidence"

Does Not Become

"Arrogance"

YOUR THOUGHTS

BACKUP POWER: PSALM 51:10 NIV

Scripture: Psalm 51:10 NIV

Create in me a clean heart, O God, and renew a steadfast spirit within me.

How can you ensure that you are keeping your heart and mind in the right place?

_____
_____
_____
_____
_____
_____
_____
_____
_____
_____
_____
_____
_____

Day 6

PEN AND PAPER

If you were given a piece of paper and were told that whatever you write down will be granted...
What Would You Say?
(Note: There Are No Wrong Answers)

YOUR THOUGHTS

BACKUP POWER: HABAKKUK 2: 2-3 MSG

Scripture: Habakkuk 2:2-3 MSG

And then God answered: "Write this. Write what you see."
Write it out in big block letters so that it can be the reason the run.
This vision-message is a witness pointing to what's coming. It aches for the coming- it can hardly wait! And it doesn't lie. If it seems slow in coming, wait. It's on its way. It will come right on time.

What is your vision for your life? What is God saying about it?

Day 7

REALIZE THAT YOU SMELL DIFFERENT...

It's crazy how people that "KNOW" you are trying to figure out why you don't smell like the "Hell Fire" you have been through. Just let them keep thinking, while God Keeps On Blessing!

YOUR THOUGHTS

BACKUP POWER: DANIEL 3:26-27 NIV

Scripture: Daniel 3: 26-27 NIV

Nebuchadnezzar then approached the opening of the blazing furnace and shouted, "Shadrach, Meshach and Abednego, servants of the Most High God, come out! Come here!" So Shadrach, Meshach and Abednego came out of the fire, and the satraps, prefects, governors and royal advisers crowded around them. They saw that the fire had not harmed their bodies, nor was a hair of their heads singed; their robes were not scorched, and there was no smell of fire on them.

Describe how you came out of a fiery experience, alive.

Day 8

BREATHE DEEP...

BREATHE IN COURAGE
AND
EXHALE FEAR

YOUR THOUGHTS

BACKUP POWER: 2 TIMOTHY 1:7 AMP

Scripture: 2 Timothy 1:7 AMP

For God did not give us a spirit of
timidity or cowardice or fear, but He has given us a spirit
of power and of love and of sound judgment and
personal discipline abilities that result in a calm, well-balanced mind and
self-control.

How can you live life a little more courageously?

Day 9

NOW DIG DEEP

Flowers are beautiful, but the reason for their beauty is in the root.
The root is buried deep underground.
That's where you have to go, deep inside of yourself,
and bring out your best every day.
Some days may be harder than others but keep going and don't stop!

YOUR THOUGHTS

BACKUP POWER: PSALM 37: 23-24 NIV

Scripture: Psalm 37: 23-24 NIV

The Lord makes firm the steps of the one
who delights in him; though he may
stumble, he will not fall,
for the Lord upholds him with his hand.

How can you challenge yourself to dig deep, and trust the Lord has got you?

Day 10

YOU ARE NOT LEFTOVERS...

You Are A Main Course.
Stop Treating Yourself, and Stop Letting Others Treat You Like Scraps.
You Were Created To Be Great and Not An Afterthought.

YOUR THOUGHTS

BACKUP POWER: LUKE 12:7 NLV

Scripture: Luke 12:7 NLV

Indeed, the very hairs of your head are
all numbered.
Don't be afraid; you are worth more than many sparrows.

What are a few of your unique, greatest God-given characteristics?

Intermission

Hey, guess what you are 10 Days into "Bringing Out The Roar". My hope and my prayers are that you are strengthened by what you are reading and what you have written down for yourself.

I hope that you feel your "Roar" getting stronger by the day... So Let's get ready to jump back in for Day 11, I will talk to you again soon!!!

Day 11

SO WHAT YOUR CROWN IS LEANING…

People are waiting in the shadows hoping you fall, but they didn't realize that God built you to "Lean and not Fall". Let them keep looking because you're on the rise. with Christ walking into your next miracle!!!

YOUR THOUGHTS

BACKUP POWER: ROMANS 8:28 NIV

Scripture: Romans 8:28 NIV

And we know that in all things God works
for the good of those who love him, who have been called according to his purpose.

Reflect on a time when your setback was really just a setup for your next level.

Day 12

INTENTIONALLY L♡VE YOURSELF...

*Take time out every day and love yourself.
Give yourself gentle reminders that you love: The Progress,
The Process, How Far You Have Come and Where You Are Going*

YOUR THOUGHTS

PROVERBS 19:8; PSALM 139:14 NIV

Scripture: Proverbs 19:8; Psalm 139:14 NIV

The one who gets wisdom loves life;
the one who cherishes understanding will soon prosper.
I praise you because I am fearfully and wonderfully made;
your works are wonderful,
I know that full well.

How are you going to take time to live your life and love yourself?

Day 13

BE AWARE OF BASIC BUYERS...

Some people want you to stay the same and not grow "Up" past them. They know your growth will soon make their "Role" diminished in your life. You can try to help, but don't let them reel you into staying basic.
There's a Bigger place for you and God wants to take you there.

YOUR THOUGHTS

BACKUP POWER: JEREMIAH 29:11 NIV

Scripture: Jeremiah 29:11 NIV

For I know the plans I have for you," declares the Lord, "plans to prosper you and not to harm you, plans to give you hope and a future.

How can you keep yourself from becoming "Basic"? How will you assess your worth?

Day 14

EVALUATION DAY...

Take time to reflect on this stage of life and evaluate who cares and who really cares. GOD is the one that really cares, you need to know that you are #Essential to Him today, tomorrow, and beyond.
Work on being your best you through Him.

YOUR THOUGHTS

BACKUP POWER: JOHN 3:16 NIV

Scripture: John 3:16 NIV

For God so loved the world that he gave
his one and only Son, that whoever believes in him
shall not perish but have eternal life.

Reflect on this passage and write down what it means to you.

Half-Time

Guess What??? You are now 15 Days into "Bringing Out The Roar". I hope that you are powering through with the daily inspirations, and your personal reflections.

**Starting with Day 15...
I want you to continue to keep pushing forward and "Bringing Out That Roar". Don't worry, you are not alone because God has you!!!**

Day 15

LOOK BACK BUT DON'T STAY...

Occasionally we will all get a gentle reminder the Lord gives that shows you how far you have come! You have come a long way in this lifetime. Every once in a while, God will give a "Flashback Reminder" on how far He has brought you and a preview of where you are going. #TRUSTTHEPROCESS

YOUR THOUGHTS

BACKUP POWER: PSALM 37: 23-24 NIV

Scripture: Psalm 37:23-24 NIV

The Lord makes firm the steps of the one
who delights in him; though he may stumble, he will not fall,
for the Lord upholds him with his hand.

Remember a time when you stumbled and yet God held you together.

Scripture: Psalm 37:23-24 NIV

The Lord makes firm the steps of the one
who delights in him; though he may stumble, he will not fall,
for the Lord upholds him with his hand.

Remember a time when you stumbled and yet God held you together.

Day 16

OWN IT...

Guess What??? It's yours...
The Blessings... They are Yours
The Breakthroughs... They are Yours
The Miracles...They are Yours...
Receive The Blessing, Grab That Breakthrough & Own The Miracle.

YOUR THOUGHTS

BACKUP POWER: GENESIS 32:26-28 NIV

Scripture: Genesis 32:26-28 NIV

Then the man said, "Let me go, for it is daybreak."
But Jacob replied, "I will not let you go unless you bless me."
The man asked him, "What is your name?" "Jacob," he answered.
Then the man said, "Your name will no longer be Jacob, but Israel,
because you have struggled with God and with humans and have overcome."

What blessings are you expecting?

_____
_____
_____
_____
_____
_____
_____
_____
_____
_____
_____
_____
_____
_____

Day 17

DON'T LET 20/20 BLOCK YOUR BLESSING...

Your eyesight will only allow you to see what's in front of you. But once you get passed the visibe, what are you going to do next??? Exercise your Faith and know that what your thought was the end is only the beginning of your next level.

YOUR THOUGHTS

BACKUP POWER: 2 COR. 5:7 AMP

Scripture: 2 Cor. 5:7 AMP

Now He who has made us and prepared us for this very purpose is God, who gave us the Holy Spirit as a pledge a guarantee, a down payment on the fulfillment of His promise. So then, being always filled with good courage and confident hope, and
knowing that while we are at home in the body we are absent from the Lord— for we walk by faith, not by sight living our lives in a manner consistent with our confident belief in God's promises.

How are your thoughts preparing you for what's next?

Day 18

KEEP GOING...

*Your eyesight will only allow you to see
what's in front of you.
But once you get past the visible,
what are you going to do next???
Exercise your faith and know that what you thought was
the end is only the beginning of your next level.*

YOUR THOUGHTS

BACKUP POWER: JOB 17:9 MSG

Scripture: JOB 17:9 MSG

The righteous keep moving forward, and
those with clean hands become stronger and stronger.

What obstacles will you have to overcome to keep going and move forward?

Day 19

IT'S WORKING OUT

Trust God's Timing... It's difficult to just stand when you are ready to abandon ship. But honestly, the blessing is in standing when you Don't Feel Like It. God is working it out just for you!

YOUR THOUGHTS

BACKUP POWER: PSALM 26:6-12 ESV

Scripture: Psalm 26:6-12

I wash my hands in innocence and go around your altar, O Lord, proclaiming thanksgiving aloud and
telling all your wondrous deeds. O Lord, I love the habitation of your house and the place where your glory dwells. Do not sweep my soul away with sinners, nor my life with bloodthirsty men, in whose hands are evil devices, and whose right hand are full of bribes. But as for me, I shall walk in my integrity; redeem me, and be gracious to me. My foot stands on level ground; in the great assembly I will bless the Lord.

What are some barriers that keep you from believing God is working it out?

Day 20

STOP and Reflect

Guess What??? You are now 20 Days into "Bringing Out The Roar".
I want you to think about where you started and where you are now.
Starting with Day 20...
I want you to continue to keep pushing forward and "Bringing Out That Roar". Don't worry, you are not alone because God has you!!! You Are Great and You Are Made For This Moment.

Day 21

DON'T GET FUNKY WITH FOLKS!!!

Humility Is Key!!!

Don't be so quick to put yourself on a pedestal.

God will easily flip your situation and now you are starting over.

Stay Humble In All That You Do!!!

YOUR THOUGHTS

BACKUP POWER: 1 PETER 5:6 ESV

Scripture: 1 Peter 5:6 ESV

Humble yourselves,
therefore, under the mighty hand of God so that at the proper time he may exalt you.

What are some practical things you can do to keep yourself from getting too proud? How do you plan to stay humble amidst great success?

Day 22

SOME THINGS STILL HURT

*Absolutely it still hurts, for some it's been 30+ years of pain.
But, why do you think you are still here.
You're Not A Mistake and You're Loved
Please Understand "Broken Crayons Still Color!!"*

YOUR THOUGHTS

_____
_____
_____
_____
_____
_____
_____
_____
_____
_____
_____
_____

BACKUP POWER: HEBREWS 12:1 NIV

Scripture: Hebrews 12:1 NIV

Therefore, since we are surrounded by such a great cloud of witnesses, let us throw off everything that hinders and the sin that so easily entangles. And let us run with perseverance the race marked out for us.

What are the major weights in your life that keep you from enjoying true freedom?

Day 23

OH MY...

When God gives you a flashback of how far you have come,
You Just Cry and Say Thank You, Jesus!!!
You are Where You Need To Be For Now,
Its Preperation For Where You Are Going!

YOUR THOUGHTS

BACKUP POWER: 1 CORINTHIANS 15:57 NIV

Scripture: I Corinthians 15:57 NIV

But thanks be to God! He
gives us the victory through our Lord Jesus Christ.

Reflect on a time when God really surprised
you with His goodness and provision.

Day 24

BE STRATEGIC MOVING FORWARD!!!

There are 300+ Billion different combinations for your first four moves in a game of chess. Don't beat yourself up if it was not right the first time. Everyday keep showing up for yourself, work everyday to trust God in All The Steps You Make.

YOUR THOUGHTS

BACKUP POWER: MATTHEW 6:25-27 NIV

Scripture: Matthew 6:25-27 NIV

Therefore I tell you, do not worry about your life, what you will eat or drink; or about your body, what you will wear. Is not life more than food, and the body more than clothes? Look
at the birds of the air; they do not sow or reap or store away in barns, and yet your heavenly Father feeds them. Are you not much more valuable than they?
Can any one of you by worrying add a single hour to your life?

Is it difficult for you not to worry about your problems and the future? If so, why?

21+

No, this is not the Adult side of the Journal, but the Congratulations side of the Journal. Congratulations because in 21+ days you formed a "Habit" of wanting to "Bring Out Your Roar". Now let's finish what you started.

You chose 21+ days ago to become great this year, so do not let the the world's actions, opinions, thoughts or even your own self-doubt stop you from achieving greatness for yourself and your family.
Remember:

"You Can Do All Things Through Christ Jesus"

Day 25

NO WON'T STOP YOU...

When we hear the word no, for some it's a death blow. They just stop what they are doing and change their course. Allow God to tap into your Greatness. Let the "No" be your pause and regroup moment.

YOUR THOUGHTS

BACKUP POWER: DEUTERONOMY 31:6,8 NIV

Scripture: Deuteronomy 31:6,8 NIV

Be strong and courageous. Do not be afraid or terrified because of them, for the Lord your God goes with you; he will never leave you nor forsake you." The Lord himself goes before you and will be with you; he will never leave you nor forsake you. Do not be afraid; do not be discouraged."

To what extent do you allow Fear to control you? What can you do to intentionally live more courageously?

_____
_____
_____
_____
_____
_____
_____
_____
_____
_____
_____
_____
_____
_____

Day 26

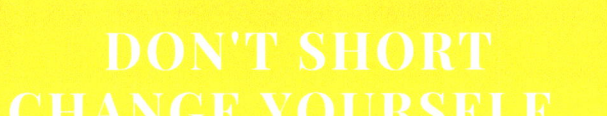

DON'T SHORT CHANGE YOURSELF...

Would you prefer the house or the neighborhood? You are built to have the best and not settle for less. A house is great, but God created you to own the community. Reach for whatever it is, Grab It A Hold of It, and Don't Let Go!!!

YOUR THOUGHTS

BACKUP POWER: MATTHEW 6:33 ESV

Scripture: Matthew 6:33 ESV

But seek first the kingdom
of God and his righteousness, and all these things will be
added to you.

What are you believing God for? Are your dreams BIG enough?

Day 21

TICK TOCK

The clock is ticking, but patience is your best friend. You know what you want, but God knows the time to release your blessing.
They that Wait upon the Lord shall renew their Strength!

YOUR THOUGHTS

BACKUP POWER: ISAIAH 40:31 NKJV

Scripture: Isaiah 40:31 NKJV

But those who wait on the Lord
Shall renew their strength; They shall mount up with wings like eagles, They shall run and not be weary, They shall walk and not faint.

What are the benefits of exercising patience? How would it improve your natural and spiritual life?

Day 28

CHOICES...

We make choices every day to do things that seem correct...

Make A Decision To Make The Right Decision For Your Life...

YOUR THOUGHTS

BACKUP POWER: ROMANS 12:2 ESV

Scripture: Romans 12:2 ESV

Do not be conformed to this world, but be transformed by the renewal of your mind, that by testing you may discern what is the will of God, what is good and acceptable and perfect.

How are your choices currently affecting your life? Are they in line with the will of God for you?

_____
_____
_____
_____
_____
_____
_____
_____
_____
_____
_____
_____
_____
_____

Day 29

WOW...

It's So Amazing How God Gives Us Reminders Of
How We Are Loved By Him...
Those times when we want to let go, throw in the towel, or even
feel worthless. Gods gentle reminders of love
"Show Up and Deliver" right on time!!

YOUR THOUGHTS

BACKUP POWER: ROMANS 5:8 ESV

Scripture: Romans 5:8 ESV

But God shows his love for
us in that while we were still sinners, Christ died for us.

How does it feel to know that Jesus still loved you
enough to die for you, even on your worst day?

Day 30

WATCH THE MIRROR

Remember there's someone that looks up to you and there's someone who's counting on you to keep going. Just in case you don't think so... Take a look in the mirror...
You're On The Next Page...

YOUR THOUGHTS

BACKUP POWER: GALATIANS 2:20 ESV

Scripture: Galations 2:20 ESV

I have been crucified with Christ. It is no longer I who live, but Christ who lives in me. And the life I now live in the flesh I live by faith in the Son of God, who loved me and gave himself for me.

What is your motivation to keep improving the person you see in the mirror? Who are you living your life to please?

Take A Look In The Mirror

Place Your Photo or
One That Has
Inspired This Journey

Additional Notes:

www.ingramcontent.com/pod-product-compliance
Lightning Source LLC
Chambersburg PA
CBHW042334150426
43194CB00005B/162